2 The Natural Balance

4 Living the Alkaline Way

6 Balanced Foods

8 Power Week

10 Breakfasts & Drinks

22 Salads & Dips

38 From the Pan, Pot, & Oven

54 Desserts

60 Index

D1466890

The Natural
between acid and alkaline
Balance

ACID, ALKALINE, AND pH

Do you sometimes feel "sour" – even "acidic"? Or do you simply feel worn out? The reason for this could be a less-than-ideal balance between acid and alkaline elements in your body. Chemically speaking, an acid always contains the free, positively charged water particles: H+. An alkali consists mainly of negatively charged particles with a single water atom and a single oxygen atom: OH-. The level of acid and alkaline is measured in pH. If this figure is 7, the positively and negatively charged particles are balanced, or neutral. The alkaline level rises from 7 to 14, and the acid level falls from 7 to 0.

ACID AND ALKALINE IN THE BODY

The pH values in our bodies differ from organ to organ. This is because certain reactions occur only at a specific pH level. In the stomach, where hydrochloric acid is produced, the pH value is very acid. The gall bladder and pancreas also produce acids. Alkaline digestive juices are produced solely in the saliva and in the duodenum. The pH value can vary tremendously throughout our connective tissue, but it must remain more or less stable at 7.4 in the blood–slightly alkaline; otherwise our metabolism would break down. Our body has a buffer system to ensure it stays at the desired alkaline level, no matter how well or how poorly we eat. By constantly discharging acids through the lungs, kidneys, digestive organs, and skin, our bodies maintain the proper acid-alkaline balance.

IF THE BALANCE IS WRONG

In a healthy body, acid and alkaline are well balanced. However, stress, unhealthy eating, and too little rest and relaxation can have such an effect on this balance that we start to feel unwell. Our modern lifestyles tend to increase the production of acid in the body: fast food, high-protein foods (such as meat, cheese, and fish), sweets, alcohol, coffee, and tobacco, all produce large amounts of acid. To make things worse, we rush around all day, neglect to breathe properly or get enough exercise, and do not eat enough alkaline forming foods to help our bodies achieve the proper balance.

DO I HAVE TOO MUCH ACID?

Because our bodies have such good buffers, we never really become overly "acidic." However, latent over-acidity can become a chronic condition and, in time, put our bodies under great stress. Excessive acid can accumulate in the tissues, where it is difficult to find, but it still makes its presence known. The circulation diminishes, and tissues become slack. The body itself soon shows the symptoms of over-acidity; frequent heartburn, gastritis, exhaustion, backache, a "spongy" feel to the skin, and brittle hair and fingernails are all typical signs.

HOW TO FIND OUT FOR YOURSELF

The pH content of the urine changes throughout the course of a day. It is affected by the amount of sleep we get, as well as by what we eat and drink. Ideally, the pH level of our urine should be somewhere between 5 and 8. Urine is generally more acidic in the morning and evening, and more alkaline at midday and in the afternoon. To get an idea of your internal chemistry, you can measure the acidity in your urine before and after every meal and before you go to bed. You can find the test strips at your local drugstore. On contact with urine, the strips will change color at a pH level between 5 and 8. If the figures are outside this range, follow our "Power Week" eating plan (see pages 8-9), and measure again at the end of the seven-day period. The best proof, however, is how much better you'll feel after changing to an alkaline-forming diet. The principles laid out in the plan can be incorporated into your eating plan for life.

Living the
What works – and how
Alkaline Way

Food's Potential

Depending on its composition, all food that we eat produces a certain amount of acidic or alkaline substances in our bodies. For example, protein is highly acid forming, carbohydrates are alkaline forming, and fats are neutral. Minerals too, can be positively or negatively charged, and affect the acid or alkaline balance in the body. The processes of the digestive system also contribute to the end result of acid or alkaline balance. Determining the acid- or alkaline-forming potential of a particular food is not foolproof. However, the tables on pages 6 and 7 can be used as a rough guide.

Acid-Forming Substances

Many foods and drinks that we consume to rev up our systems actually cause our bodies' pH level to drop; for example, alcohol, coffee, soda, and improperly brewed tea can all cause excess acid in the system. Chocolate, candy, cakes, cookies, refined sugar, and white flour are also acid forming. Consuming meats, fish, shellfish, cheese, and eggs also lead to a buildup of acid in the system. Conversely, a vegetarian diet is highly alkaline promoting.

The Neutrals

Our bodies need neutral substances because they contain vital nutrients. Neutral foods include cultured milk products and milk with added calcium. Butter, clarified butter, and cold-pressed oils with added vitamin E and beta-carotene are also neutral substances. Amaranth, spelt, millet, quinoa, and buckwheat are all full of protein and vitamin B, and are an ideal substitute for the more common types of grains, as well as acid-forming rice.

Beneficial Alkaline forming Foods

With just a few exceptions, fruit, potatoes, and vegetables are highly alkaline. Even if some foods taste acidic, such as citrus fruits, they can have an alkaline effect on the body. This also applies to vegetables that contain lactic acid, such as sauerkraut.

There are vast differences between the different types of legumes; although flageolet beans are alkaline forming, most dried legumes are acid forming. Opinions differ with regard to nuts and seeds, but almonds, pumpkin seeds, and sunflower seeds are alkaline forming—and the fresher they are, the better.

Note: Sprouts are always alkaline, and therefore very healthy. Furthermore, fresh sprouts are full of vitamins, minerals, and bioactive substances.

WHAT SHOULD I DRINK?

It's important to make sure you drink enough fluids, as they are beneficial for the kidneys and help the body to flush away acids. Ideally, you should drink at least 2 quarts of liquid per day. Noncarbonated mineral water is a good choice, as are mild herbal teas. Special alkaline-forming teas are sold in health food stores. Black tea, provided it is left to brew for at least four minutes, is a sound choice. Natural fruit and vegetable juices are alkaline forming, but almost count as a snack, and are best diluted with water. Among milk products, choose buttermilk or acidopholous milk.

WHAT ABOUT SNACKS?

Constantly adding undigested food to the semi-digested food already in our stomach can cause heartburn and over-acidity. It is therefore better to stick to three meals a day, with perhaps a little fruit in between if you are really hungry. Low-fat granola and salads are ideal, alkaline-forming cold meals. Sandwich ingredients, however, are usually highly acid forming. Instead, opt for some Spelt and Potato Bread with a vegetarian spread (see pages 16–17).

Balanced

foods to remember for a balanced diet

Foods

Several factors determine whether a food is acid- or alkaline-forming, such as its mineral content, its effect on the body's metabolic system, and its effects on the digestive organs. The following table is intended as a guideline.

NOTE: To achieve and maintain the ideal balance, the food you eat should be 80 percent alkaline forming and 20 percent acid forming. Eat neutral foods in moderation, and choose those that are low-fat.

REMEMBER: Foods that taste acidic don't necessarily have an acidic effect on the body. Citrus fruit, kiwi, and pineapple are, like most fruits, highly alkaline forming. Vegetables that contain lactic acid, such as sauerkraut, capers, pickled gherkins, and olives, are alkaline forming even though they taste acidic.

ALKALINE FORMING

potatoes

most fresh vegetables

fresh fruit

dried fruit

honey

fruit syrups

maple syrup

cane sugar

sprouts & seeds

herbs and spices (cinnamon, bay leaves, vanilla, marjoram, dill, mustard, cumin)

sauerkraut

capers

olives

yeast

soy sauce

herbal teas

noncarbonated water

NEUTRAL TO SLIGHTLY ALKALINE FORMING

milk

acidopholous milk

buttermilk

yogurt

cream

soy milk

tofu

millet

buckwheat

amaranth

quinoa

potato flour

arrowroot

egg yolks

butter

cold-pressed oils

vinegar

sunflower seeds

pumpkin seeds

NEUTRAL TO SLIGHTLY ACID FORMING

spelt

whole-grain crackers

sourdough bread

green beans

brown rice

sesame seeds

cashew nuts

pistachios

almonds

hazelnuts

fresh cheeses

cottage cheese

sour milk products

beer

dry wine

ACID FORMING

meats and sausages

fish

shellfish

egg whites

aged cheese

white flour

light-colored breads

pasta

rice

corn

refined sugar

chocolate

candy

peanuts

walnuts

Brussels sprouts

artichokes

carbonated drinks

alcoholic beverages

coffee

black tea (brewed for less than one minute)

Power
Eating and drinking the alkaline way
Week

CHANGE THE HABITS OF A LIFETIME

Do life's stresses make you feel like escaping to a desert island? Instead, try this basic eating plan for a week, and see if you still feel the same way at the end of it. Excess acid will be eliminated from your body and you will soon start to feel fit and relaxed. It could be the beginning of a new, healthier way of life. In time, you can gradually re-introduce dairy products and normal grains to your diet. If you decide to follow this plan for the long term, be sure to take calcium supplements.

THE ONE-WEEK BALANCING PLAN

The weekend before you start, bake some Spelt and Potato Bread*, make some Potato and Almond Spread and Mixed Fruit Puree, and prepare some Vegetable Stock. Buy the ingredients for Ginger and Nettle Tisane, and a mountain of fruit. Drink at least 2 quarts of spring water, and as much vegetable stock as you like every day. You can also prepare for the week by eating only fruit and vegetables on the Sunday before you begin the plan to detoxify your system. In the Power Week's plan, there are three main meals per day and two "extras," which you can eat either at mealtimes or as snacks in between; make sure you leave at least two hours between meals. Incidentally, you may experience headaches and weariness, and generally feel down when you first begin the plan. Hold out—in no time you'll start to feel better. And last, but not least: if you find you are still hungry after a meal, eat twice the amount next time.

❋ Hint: Freeze the bread in portions so that it remains fresh all week.

THE WEEK'S MEALS

Monday

- 1 slice of Spelt and Potato Bread with Potato and Almond Spread; Mixed Fruit Puree
- Curried Potato Pancake Buckwheat-Stuffed Tomatoes with 2 slices of Spelt and Potato Bread Berry Milkshake

Tuesday

- Muesli with Spelt and Millet Winter Bean Stew Arugula and Wild Rice Salad with 1 slice of Spelt and Potato Bread Pumpkin Salsa Verde with raw or steamed vegetables

Wednesday

- 2 slices of Spelt and Potato Bread with Potato and Almond Spread and butter; Mixed Fruit Puree or honey Potato and Tomato Cocktail; Fresh Plum Dumplings Roasted Fennel with Exotic Mushrooms; boiled new potatoes and Quinoa and Butter Lettuce Salad Pear Milkshake with Cinnamon

Thursday

- Mixed Fruit Granola Creamy Asparagus Dip with boiled new potatoes
- Provençal Vegetable Salad with 2 slices of Spelt and Potato Bread
- Cream of Basil Soup

Friday

- Muesli with Fresh Berries 1 slice of Spelt and Potato Bread with Potato and Almond Spread or Honeyed Fresh Fruit Potato-Apple Gratin; Dandelion Salad with Kidney Beans and 1 slice of Spelt and Potato Bread Chocolate Pudding

Saturday

- 1–2 slices of Spelt and Potato Bread with Honeyed Fresh Fruit; Berry Milkshake
- Vegetable Tempura with tomato sauce; Marinated Peppers Green Pasta Salad with Potato and Tomato Cocktail Red Currant Sorbet Float

Sunday

- 1–2 slices of Spelt and Potato Bread with Honeyed Fresh Fruit; Potato and Almond Spread Beet Ragout; Tomato and Asparagus Salad Cream of Pumpkin Soup

Honeyed

also delicious with

Fresh

citrus fruits

Fruit

Serves 4: 1/3 cup honey • 1 kiwi • 1 nectarine • 1 tbs fresh lemon juice • 4 oz fresh strawberries or raspberries • 2 tbs fresh blueberries

Spread 2–3 tablespoons of the honey over the bottom of a flat dish. Peel the kiwi and cut into 1/4-inch slices. Slice the nectarine and sprinkle with lemon juice. Pick over the berries, wash if necessary, and pat dry. Spread the fruit over the honey and cover with the remaining honey. The fruit will keep for 1 week if stored in an airtight container in the refrigerator.

TOTAL: 123 calories • 1 g protein • 1 g fat • 32 g carbohydrates

Ginger and Nettle
diuretic, invigorating, and alkaline forming
Tisane with Licorice

Makes about 1 quart: 1 finger-sized piece fresh ginger • 1 piece licorice root • 3 tbs nettle tea • Freshly ground nutmeg to taste • 1 quart boiling water • 1 orange

Finely chop the ginger and licorice and place in a teapot with the tea and some freshly ground nutmeg. Pour over the boiling water and let steep for 10 minutes. Wash the orange, cut it into slices, and place in heat-resistant glasses. Strain the tisane over the orange slices. Drink the tisane hot or cold.

TOTAL: 18 calories • 0 g protein • 1 g fat • 4 g carbohydrates

Berry
flavored with vanilla bean
Milkshake

Serves 2: 4 oz berries (fresh or frozen) • 1 cup cold acidopholous milk • 1 vanilla bean • 1-2 tbs fruit syrup or honey

Sort and wash the berries, then drain. Place in a blender with the milk. Slit the vanilla bean open. Using a sharp knife, scrape the seeds from the pod and add to the berry mixture. Add the syrup or honey and blend all the ingredients well. Pour into tall glasses and serve with straws.

PER DRINK: 130 calories • 5 g protein • 3 g fat • 23 g carbohydrates

Pear Milkshake

mild tasting and rich in calcium

with Cinnamon

Serves 2: 1 pear • 1 cup cold whole milk • 1/2 tsp ground cinnamon • 1-2 tsp floral honey

Wash and peel the pear. Cut it into quarters, and remove the core and stem. With a blender, process the pear with the milk, cinnamon, and honey until smooth. Pour into tall glasses and serve with straws.

PER DRINK: 132 calories • 5 g protein • 5 g fat • 21 g carbohydrates

Potato and Tomato

with acid-binding potato juice

Cocktail

Serves 2: 1 lb potatoes, or 1/2 cup potato juice • 1 tbs cider vinegar • 2 fresh basil leaves • 2 tbs capers with liquid • 1 cup tomato juice • Pinch of herbed salt mix • Black pepper

Wash, peel, and puree the potatoes. Sprinkle the vinegar over the potatoes and let stand for 10 minutes before passing through a fine sieve; Or, combine the potato juice and vinegar. Wash the basil leaves and pat dry. Finely chop the capers and basil leaves. Combine with the potato mixture, tomato juice, salt, and pepper. Serve immediately in cocktail glasses.

PER DRINK: 72 calories • 3 g protein • 1 g fat • 16 g carbohydrates

Spelt and
with alkaline-forming ingredients
Potato Bread

Wash the potatoes, and steam them for 20-30 minutes, until tender. Peel the potatoes while still hot and push through a potato ricer into a large bowl. Combine the spelt flours and the yeast, and add them gradually to the mashed potatoes, mixing well.

Makes 2 loaves:
1 lb baking potatoes
1 lb spelt flour
1 lb whole-grain spelt flour
2 packets rapid-rise yeast
Lukewarm water
2 tbs salt
1 tsp ground cumin
8 oz sunflower kernels

If the dough seems too stiff, thin it with a little water; the dough should have a soft, malleable consistency. Shape it into a ball in the bowl. Cover the bowl and let the dough rise at room temperature for 1 hour. Add the salt, cumin, and half of the sunflower kernels. Knead the dough gently to mix in the ingredients.

Grease the insides of 2 loaf pans and sprinkle with half of the remaining sunflower kernels. Divide the dough in half, place it in the pans, and sprinkle with the remaining sunflower kernels. Place the loaves in the bottom of a cold oven, turn the heat to 400°F, and bake for about 1 hour, until the loaves sound hollow when thumped. Let the loaves cool in the pans, then remove.

PER PORTION:
202 calories
8 g protein
5 g fat
31 g carbohydrates

Potato and

with fresh basil and garlic

Almond Spread

Wash the potatoes, and steam them for 20-30 minutes, until tender. Meanwhile, steep the almonds in boiling water for a few minutes, then

Makes one 10-oz jar:
8 oz baking potatoes
2 oz whole almonds
1 bunch fresh basil
1 clove garlic
4-5 tbs olive oil
1 tsp salt
Black pepper to taste

rinse in cold water and remove the skins. Wash the basil, shake dry, and tear off the leaves. Peel and crush the garlic. Puree the almonds, olive oil, basil, garlic, salt, and pepper with a blender or food processor until smooth.

Peel the hot potatoes and blend to a paste with the basil-almond mixture. Add salt and pepper to taste. The spread will keep for 3-4 days in a tightly capped jar in the refrigerator.

Potatoes

In folk medicine, potatoes are regarded as a universal panacea. Although highly alkaline, they are full of protein. Grain protein is an ideal accompaniment, so bread topped with this savory potato spread can definitely hold its own against a steak sandwich. To retain their nutrients, potatoes are best steamed in their skins, rather than peeled and boiled.

TOTAL:

830 calories

16 g protein

68 g fat

42 g carbohydrates

Mixed Fruit

contains no acid-forming sugar

Puree

Makes one 10-oz jar: 4 oz pitted prunes • 4 oz raisins • 4 oz dried figs • 1/2 cup orange juice

• Ground cinnamon to taste

Wash the prunes, raisins, and figs in hot water, drain on paper towels, and chop. Place in a bowl, pour over the orange juice, and let stand for 1 hour. Puree the mixture in a blender and season with cinnamon. Store in the refrigerator in an airtight container. Keeps for up to 2 weeks.

TOTAL: 800 calories • 9 g protein • 3 g fat • 193 g carbohydrates

Uncooked Mixed-

alkaline forming when sweetened with honey

Fruit Jam

Makes one 10-oz jar: 8 oz red currants • 4 oz strawberries • 1/4-1/2 cup honey

Pick over and wash the red currants and strawberries, and drain them thoroughly. Strip the currants from the stalks and press them through a coarse sieve. Cut any large strawberries into smaller pieces. Beat the red currant puree, strawberries, and honey to taste in an electric mixer for 10 minutes, until the mixture begins to thicken. Store in a tightly capped sterilized jar in a cool, dark place. Keeps for 4-6 weeks.

TOTAL: 576 calories • 3 g protein • 1 g fat • 138 g carbohydrates

Muesli with Spelt
with tangy citrus
and Millet

Place the grains and poppy seeds in a saucepan with the water and simmer gently for 1 minute. Cool, then chill until ready to use.

Serves 2:
3 tbs coarsely ground spelt
3 tbs coarsely ground millet
2 tbs poppy seeds
1 cup water
1 small banana
1 cup milk
1 pink grapefruit
1 orange

Peel the banana, blend with the milk, and combine with the grains. Divide the grain and milk mixture among two bowls.

Peel the grapefruit and orange with a very sharp knife, removing all of the bitter white pith. Cut down the sides of each membrane to release the fruit segments. Arrange the fruit pieces on the muesli and serve immediately.

Grains

As well as good quantities of fiber, vitamins, and bioactive substances, grains also contain *phytin*, an acid that prevents minerals and–probably–vitamins from being absorbed in the digestive tract. Phytin loses its efficacy when cooked, baked, or sprouted, which is why freshly ground or flaked cereals should be both boiled and soaked before eating. Ready-flaked cereals have already been cooked.

PER PORTION:

272 calories

10 g protein

7 g fat

43 g carbohydrates

power

Mixed Fruit
with popped amaranth
Granola

Wash and peel the apple. Cut it in half and remove the core, then chop into small pieces. Wash the figs and apricots, drain, and chop into small

Serves 2:
1 large apple
2 dried figs
6 dried apricots
1 cup water
1 cinnamon stick
1-2 tbs honey
8 tbs popped amaranth

pieces. Place the figs and apricots in a saucepan with the apple, water, and cinnamon and bring to a boil. Simmer gently, covered, for about 5 minutes. Stir in the honey. Let the apple puree cool and remove the cinnamon stick. Divide the apple puree among two dishes and serve immediately topped with the popped amaranth.

Amaranth

Amaranth, a seed from the Andes, is less acid forming than many other grains and is high in protein. Since it contains no gluten, it is not suitable for baking with yeast, unless combined with wheat flours. Amaranth is available popped from specialty and health food stores. It is also available in whole-grain form, which can be ground either in the store or, if you prefer, by yourself at home.

PER PORTION:

282 calories

5 g protein

3 g fat

65 g carbohydrates

Sprouted Muesli
invigorating and low in calories
with Fresh Berries

Place the seeds in a preserving jar, cover with warm water, and soak for 24 hours. Drain the seeds, rinse, and return to the jar. Fill the jar with water and let stand for a few minutes. Cover the jar with a double layer of cheesecloth and secure with a rubber band. Place the jar upside down on a rack in the sink to allow the water to drain away. Set the jar aside and let stand for about 5 days, until the seeds form small shoots and delicate sprouts appear.

Sprinkle the sprouts with water daily. When relatively large, wash the sprouted seeds thoroughly and drain.

Pick over and wash the berries, then drain. Combine the berries with the tiny millet shoots. Combine the yogurt and maple syrup, mixing until smooth and creamy, then pour over the berry-sprout mixture.

Serves 2:

4 oz millet seeds (easy sprouting)

1 cup fresh seasonal berries

2/3 cup plain yogurt

1-2 tbs maple syrup

Sprouted seeds

Sprouting reduces the amount of fat and *phytin* and increases the vitamin and mineral content of seeds. Sprouted seeds are less acid forming than unsprouted seeds and are perfectly digestible when raw. Wash the sprouts thoroughly in a sieve before eating. You can also stir-fry them or blanch them in boiling water.

PER PORTION:

193 calories

6 g protein

4 g fat

34 g carbohydrates

Arugula and Wild Rice Salad

a lovely dinner, snack, or brown-bag lunch

Peel and finely chop the ginger and onion. Rinse the lime under hot water, pat dry, and carefully remove the zest in strips, avoiding the white pith; set aside. Squeeze the juice from the lime. Mix the lime juice with a drop of honey, some pepper, and the green peppercorns. Marinate the onion and ginger in the lime mixture overnight.

Place the wild rice in a saucepan with the water, salt, cumin, and reserved lime zest, and bring to a boil. Simmer over low heat for 45 minutes. Let cool, then remove the zest.

Wash the arugula and cut into bite-sized pieces; wash and slice the radishes. Place the wild rice, arugula, and radishes in a bowl. Stir together the ginger-onion mixture and the oil, season to taste with salt and pepper, and pour over the salad, tossing well. Arrange the salad on plates and serve.

Serves 2:
1 piece fresh ginger (thumb-sized)
1 red onion
1 lime
Honey to taste
Pepper to taste
1 tsp green peppercorns
1/2 cup wild rice
1 cup water
Salt to taste
1/2 tsp ground cumin
1 bunch arugula
1 bunch radishes
3-4 tbs canola oil

power

PER PORTION: 350 calories • 9 g protein • 17 g fat • 44 g carbohydrates

Quinoa and

with mushrooms and horseradish

Butter Lettuce Salad

Serves 2:
- 3/4 cup quinoa
- 2 tbs olive oil
- 1/2 cup vegetable stock
- 1 small bay leaf
- 1/2 tsp fresh thyme leaves
- 1/2 head butter lettuce
- 8 oz mushrooms
- 1 small onion
- 1/2 clove garlic
- 1/2 lemon
- 5 tbs heavy cream
- 1 tbs sour cream
- 1 tsp creamy-style horseradish
- Salt to taste
- Black pepper to taste

In a skillet, sauté the quinoa in 1 tbs of the oil, until toasted. Add the vegetable stock, bay leaf, and half of the thyme. Simmer gently for 15 minutes, remove from the heat, and let cool.

Wash and drain the lettuce. Wash or wipe clean the mushrooms and cut into slices.

Peel and finely chop the onion and garlic. Finely grate the lemon zest and squeeze out the juice.

To make the dressing, whip the cream until stiff. Add the sour cream and lemon juice. Season with the lemon zest, the remaining half of the thyme, the horseradish, salt, and pepper.

Heat the remaining 1 tbs oil in a skillet and sauté the onion, mushrooms, and garlic, until softened. Season with salt and pepper.

Carefully mix half of the dressing with the cooled quinoa. Divide the lettuce leaves among two plates and drizzle with the remaining dressing. Divide the quinoa among the lettuce beds. Arrange the mushroom mixture on top and serve.

PER PORTION: 528 calories • 19 g protein • 20 g fat • 66 g carbohydrates

Dandelion Salad

soothes body and mind

with Kidney Beans

Soak the beans in the water overnight. The next day, drain and rinse the beans and replace the water with a fresh supply. Add the rosemary and bay leaf and bring to a boil. Simmer the beans for 1 1/2 hours, until tender. Add the salt, and let cool.

Grate a couple pinches of orange zest. With a thin, sharp knife, peel the whole orange, removing all the bitter white pith. Cut down the sides of each membrane to release the fruit segments (make sure you collect the juice). Squeeze the juice from the 1/2 orange and set aside with the collected juice.

Wash, peel, and dice the carrots. Heat the oil in a saucepan and sauté the carrots until softened. Season to taste with salt and pepper, add a small amount of orange juice, and simmer gently for about 8 minutes, until tender.

Serves 2:

1/2 cup dried red kidney beans

2 cups cold water

1 sprig fresh rosemary

1 small bay leaf

Salt to taste

1 1/2 oranges

4 oz carrots

1 tbs vegetable oil

Pepper to taste

1 bunch fresh chives

4 oz dandelion greens

2 tbs Dijon-style mustard

1 tbs brown mustard

1/4 cup heavy cream

Wash the chives and dandelion greens. Chop the chives, and combine with the dandelion greens, orange segments, diced carrots, and drained beans. Season well. Mix the mustards and cream with the remaining orange juice and orange zest. Season with salt and pepper. Serve the dressing with the salad.

PER PORTION: 384 calories • 16 g protein • 15 g fat • 46 g carbohydrates

Tomato and
with alkaline forming mustard powder
Asparagus Salad

Wash the asparagus and snow peas. Peel the lower third of the asparagus stalks and cut the asparagus into 2-inch pieces; set the tips aside separately.

Add some salt and the lemon juice to the water and bring to a boil. Boil the lower pieces of asparagus for 5 minutes, then add the asparagus tips and the snow peas, and cook until tender-crisp, about 3-5 minutes. Drain, reserving the cooking liquid, and place in ice water to cool.

Meanwhile, wash the tomatoes and cut into eighths. Wash and shake dry the tarragon. Remove and discard the coarse stalks, and chop the rest. Pass the egg yolk through a fine sieve and combine with the mustard and enough of the asparagus cooking liquid to make a dressing. Whisk in 1 tbs of the oil, and half of the chopped tarragon. Season with salt and pepper.

Toss the tomatoes, snow peas, and drained asparagus with the dressing and arrange on plates. Break the bread into small pieces. Heat the remaining 2 tbs oil in a skillet over medium heat and sauté the bread until brown on all sides. Sprinkle over the salad. Garnish with the remaining tarragon and serve immediately.

Serves 2:
9 oz white or green asparagus
3 oz snow peas
Salt to taste
1 tbs fresh lemon juice
1/2 cup water
2 tomatoes
1/2 bunch tarragon
1 hard-cooked egg yolk
1 tsp dry mustard
3 tbs extra virgin olive oil
Pepper to taste
3-4 thin slices stale bread

PER PORTION: 172 calories • 5 g protein • 11 g fat • 14 g carbohydrates

Roasted Fennel with

with herbes de Provence

Exotic Mushrooms

Preheat the oven to 400°F. Wash the fennel and cut in half. Remove the green tops from the fennel and set aside. Place two pieces of aluminum foil, shiny side up, on the work surface, rub

Serves 2:

2 bulbs fennel (about 10 oz each)

2 tbs extra virgin olive oil, plus more for greasing foil

1/2 tsp herbes de Provence

4 oz assorted mushrooms, such as brown (cremini), oyster, and/or chanterelle

2 tbs fresh lemon juice

1 clove garlic

1/4 cup dry white wine

Salt to taste

Black pepper to taste

with oil, and sprinkle with the herbs. Place two fennel halves, cut side down, on each piece of foil. Firmly seal the foil over the top of the fennel. Roast in the center of the oven for 35 minutes, until tender.

Wash and finely slice the mushrooms and sprinkle with 1 tsp of the lemon juice. Peel and thinly slice the garlic. Heat 1 tbs of the oil in a skillet over medium-high heat and sauté the mushrooms until tender. Add the wine, heat through, and transfer to a bowl.

Wipe out the skillet, add the remaining 1 tbs oil, and gently sauté the garlic. Season well with the remaining lemon juice, salt, and pepper, and combine with the mushrooms. Unwrap the fennel, cut into thin slices, and arrange on plates with the mushrooms and fennel greens. Refrigerate, covered, for 2 to 3 hours. Serve at room temperature.

Fennel

Fennel is alkaline forming and aids the body in breaking down acids. It contains 2-3 percent essential oils, which stimulate the circulation in the digestive tract and respiratory system, and strengthen the stomach, kidneys, and liver. Fennel is most effective eaten raw.

PER PORTION:

145 calories

5 g protein

8 g fat

8 g carbohydrates

Marinated
with chopped hazelnuts
Peppers

Preheat the grill to high (you can also use a broiler). Wash the peppers and pat dry. Grill the peppers (or cook on a baking sheet under the broiler), turning occasionally, until the skins turn black and start to blister on all sides. Remove the peppers from the grill and sprinkle with salt. Cover with a damp tea towel and let stand until cool enough to handle. Holding the peppers over a bowl, remove the charred skins, collecting any juice that exudes. Cut the peppers lengthwise into 8-10 pieces, removing the stalks, ribs, and seeds. Peel and roughly chop the garlic. Squeeze the lime and mix the juice with the pepper juices and the olive oil. Season well with the garlic, salt, pepper, and paprika. Add the pepper strips and marinate for at least 30 minutes.

Wash the parsley and shake dry. Remove the parsley leaves and roughly chop. Divide the marinated pepper strips among serving plates and sprinkle with the parsley and hazelnuts.

Serves 2:
1 red bell pepper
1 yellow bell pepper
1/2 green bell pepper
Salt to taste
1 clove garlic
1/2 lime
2 tbs extra virgin olive oil
White pepper to taste
Hot paprika to taste
1/2 bunch fresh Italian parsley
1 oz chopped hazelnuts

Peppers

Bell peppers are not just highly alkaline; the chemical *capsaicin*, prevalent in the pepper family, stimulates the circulation and digestion, beta carotene strengthens the body's resistance, and bioflavinoids stabilize the blood vessels.

PER PORTION:

185 calories

4 g protein

15 g fat

10 g carbohydrates

Provençal
lavender adds special flair
Vegetable Salad

Serves 2:
4 oz green beans
8 oz boiling potatoes
1/2 cup water
Salt to taste
1 zucchini
1 red bell pepper
1 red onion
1 clove garlic
3 tbs extra virgin olive oil
2 tbs white wine vinegar
Pepper to taste
1 tbs mustard
1 tbs chopped fresh lavender leaves and flowers
1 bunch fresh basil
1 small head radicchio
10 black olives (pitted)

Wash the beans and wash and peel the potatoes. Trim the beans, removing any strings. In a saucepan, bring the water and 1/2 tsp salt to a boil. Add the beans and potatoes and cook for 30 minutes, until tender. Trim the zucchini and cut into small pieces. Halve the pepper, remove the stem, ribs, and seeds, and cut the flesh into small pieces. Peel the onion and garlic and finely chop.

Mix together the olive oil, vinegar, pepper, mustard, and lavender. Add some of the vegetable cooking water to the dressing and season to taste.

Peel and slice the potatoes. In a bowl, pour the dressing over the potatoes and beans. Stir in the zucchini, onion, and garlic, and chill. Wash the basil and shake it dry. Pull the leaves from the stalks and tear them into rough pieces.

Cut the radicchio into bite-sized pieces. Wash and drain well. Add the basil, olives, and radicchio to the salad. Toss and season well.

PER PORTION: 335 calories • 10 g protein • 15 g fat • 45 g carbohydrates

Green

revitalizing and highly alkaline

Pasta Salad

Cook the pasta in a large amount of boiling salted water until slightly firm to the bite (al dente). Drain and rinse under cold water. Wash the spinach and the zucchini. Pick over the spinach, remove any hard stalks, and drain. Slice the zucchini thinly.

Wash the basil, shake dry, and tear off the leaves. Peel the garlic. Puree the basil leaves in a blender with the olives, stock, and lemon juice. Season the dressing with salt and pepper.

In a bowl, combine the pasta, spinach, and zucchini. Add the dressing and toss carefully. Arrange the pasta salad on 2 plates, sprinkle with the cheese, and serve.

Serves 2:
4 oz millet pasta
Salt to taste
4 oz baby spinach
5 oz zucchini
1/2 bunch fresh basil
6 green olives (pitted)
1 clove garlic
1/4 cup vegetable stock
2 tsp fresh lemon juice
Pepper to taste
1-2 tbs freshly grated
Parmesan cheese

Spinach

Spinach is one of the most alkaline-rich vegetables. It contains large amounts of iron and folic acid, and its high copper content encourages blood formation. The hormone *secretin* stimulates the pancreas. Spinach also contains oxalic acid, which binds calcium (this is what causes the rough feeling on the teeth). For maximum benefit, drink milk or calcium-enriched fruit juice when you eat spinach.

PER PORTION:
280 calories
15 g protein
8 g fat
39 g carbohydrates

Quinoa Salad with

a slightly alkaline evening meal

Creamy Vinaigrette

In a saucepan, briefly sauté the quinoa in 1 tsp of the olive oil. Add the lemon juice, water, and 1 tsp salt. Bring to a boil, cover tightly, and simmer gently for 15 minutes. Cool.

Peel and finely grate the beets. Grate the cheese coarsely. Wash the chives, shake dry, and cut into small pieces. Set aside 1/2 tsp for the dressing. Peel and finely chop the garlic. Wash and finely grate the cucumber.

In a bowl, lightly mix the quinoa, beets, cheese, chives, garlic, and cucumber. In a small bowl, combine the stock, mustard, remaining 1/2 tsp chives, pepper, vinegar, remaining 3 tsp oil, and the cream until smooth. Pour the dressing over the salad just before serving, and toss well.

Serves 2:

2/3 cup quinoa

4 tsp extra virgin olive oil

Juice of 1/2 lemon

2 cups water

Salt to taste

4 oz fresh beets, cooked

3 oz pecorino Romano cheese

1 bunch fresh chives

1 small clove garlic

1 cucumber

1/4 cup vegetable stock

1/2 tsp Dijon-style mustard

Pepper to taste

1 tbs mild vinegar

1 tbs heavy cream

Quinoa

Quinoa is a cereal-like cultivated plant from South America. Its seeds are small and round, and are slightly alkaline forming. Like amaranth, quinoa contains more protein than other grains. It is also high in iron, zinc, potassium, magnesium, and vitamin C.

PER PORTION:

409 calories

18 g protein

16 g fat

48 g carbohydrates

Buckwheat-Stuffed

full of protein and minerals

Tomatoes

Wash the tomatoes, thinly slice off the tops (to use as lids), and scoop out the insides with a spoon; reserve the insides of the tomatoes for another use. Put the tomatoes upside down in a sieve to drain. Season the tomato cavities well with salt and pepper.

Lightly toast the buckwheat groats in a nonstick skillet. Wash and thinly slice the green onions. Peel and finely chop the garlic. Chop the sauerkraut into small pieces. Wash the dill and pull the tips from the coarse stalks.

In a bowl, combine the buckwheat, green onions, garlic, sauerkraut, and dill. Add the salt, pepper, lemon juice, and oil and mix carefully. Season the filling well and divide among the tomatoes. Place the "lids" on the tomatoes, arrange on plates, and serve.

Serves 2:
6 large tomatoes (about 2 lb)
Salt to taste
Pepper to taste
1/2 cup buckwheat groats
2-3 green onions
1 clove garlic
8 oz sauerkraut (drained)
1 bunch fresh dill
3-4 tbs fresh lemon juice
2-3 tbs canola oil

Variations

Use small bell peppers instead of tomatoes. Use amaranth or quinoa for the filling instead of buckwheat (boil the grains first in 1 cup vegetable stock and cool). For a Mediterranean flair, use basil or herbes de Provence instead of dill.

PER PORTION:

441 calories

13 g protein

15 g fat

66 g carbohydrates

power

Spicy
with zesty horseradish
Radish Dip

Serves 2: 1 bunch radishes • 1/2 cup buttermilk • 1/4 cup heavy cream • 1 tsp creamy-style horseradish

• Salt to taste • Black pepper to taste

Wash the radishes and puree them in a blender, setting some of the juice aside. Mix the pureed radishes with the buttermilk. Whip the cream until stiff and combine with the radish puree. Season the dip with the horseradish, salt, and pepper. If the mixture is too thick, adjust the consistency with some of the radish juice (drink the rest) and keep the dip cool.

PER PORTION: 90 calories • 1 g protein • 8 g fat • 3 g carbohydrates

Pumpkin
with alkaline-forming olives and herbs
Salsa Verde

Serves 2: 1 bunch fresh Italian parsley • 1 bunch fresh basil • 2 oz pumpkin seeds • 2 oz green olives (pitted) • 1/2 cup vegetable stock • 2 tbs olive oil • Salt to taste • Black pepper to taste

• 1 clove garlic

Wash the herbs, shake them dry, and pull off the leaves. With a blender, puree the basil and parsley leaves with the pumpkin seeds and olives, and gradually add the stock. Mix in the oil and season with salt and pepper. Peel and finely chop the garlic and stir into the salsa.

PER PORTION: 259 calories • 10 g protein • 22 g fat • 9 g carbohydrates

Creamy
with mascarpone cheese and fresh basil
Asparagus Dip

Wash and trim the asparagus, and peel the lower third of the stalks. Wash and shake dry the basil and pull the leaves off the stems.

Place the asparagus, basil, and mascarpone in a food processor or blender and puree until the mixture is smooth and creamy.

Combine the puree with salt, pepper, lemon juice, olive oil, and a small amount of the vegetable stock, to achieve a dip consistency.

Serves 2:

4 oz asparagus

1/2 bunch fresh basil

2 oz mascarpone cheese

Salt to taste

Pepper to taste

1 tbs fresh lemon juice

1 tsp olive oil

Vegetable stock

Dips

These dips are high in protein, and go well with raw or steamed vegetables, pasta, and potatoes for a highly satisfying meal. They can easily be prepared in advance and are ideal for a brown-bag lunch.

Mascarpone has a relatively high fat content, but it is less acid forming than other types of cream cheese or cottage cheese. Its high amount of valuable lactic acid makes it slightly alkaline forming. You can increase the alkaline effect by adding vegetables to the dip–such as the asparagus used in this recipe. Asparagus is also slightly diuretic, and stimulates the liver and kidneys.

power

PER PORTION:

145 calories

3 g protein

13 g fat

5 g carbohydrates

Gnocchi
a tasty Italian-style treat
with Tomatoes

Wash the potatoes and steam them for 20-30 minutes, until very tender. Peel the potatoes while hot and push them through a potato ricer. Let stand for a few minutes to drive off the steam. Mix in 1 tsp salt, the flour, and as much potato flour as is needed until the dough is no longer sticky. On a floured work surface, shape the dough into finger-thick rolls and cut into 1-inch pieces. With a fork, slightly flatten each piece.

In a large saucepan, bring a generous amount of salted water to a boil. Reduce the heat and simmer portions of gnocchi in the water for 4 minutes. Rinse the cooked gnocchi in cold water and drain. Keep warm on a baking sheet in a very cool oven (175°F). Peel and quarter the shallots. Sauté them in a skillet with 1 tbs of the butter, cover with a lid, and simmer with the orange juice for 8 minutes, until glazed.

Serves 2:

Generous 1 lb baking potatoes

Salt to taste

3 tbs flour

2-3 tbs potato flour

3 shallots

2 tbs butter

1/4 cup orange juice

12 oz ripe tomatoes

1/2 bunch fresh sorrel

1 tbs tomato puree

Honey to taste

Mild paprika to taste

Pepper to taste

Meanwhile, cut an X into the round ends of the tomatoes and plunge them into boiling water for a few moments. Remove the skins, cut the tomatoes in half, and remove the seeds. Cut the tomato flesh into strips. Wash and pick over the sorrel and cut into strips. Add the tomato puree, honey, paprika, and the remaining 1 tbs butter to the shallots. Add the tomato strips and sorrel and heat through. Season with salt and pepper and serve with the hot gnocchi.

PER PORTION: 322 calories • 9 g protein • 6 g fat • 58 g carbohydrates

Tomato and Red
with thyme and basil
Pepper Sauce

Wash the tomatoes, remove the stalks, and cut into eighths. Cut the red pepper in half and remove the stem, ribs, and seeds. Wash it and cut it lengthwise into 4-6 pieces. Peel, halve, and chop the onion.

Serves 2:
Generous 1 lb ripe tomatoes
1 small red bell pepper
1 onion
2 tbs olive oil
1 tbs tomato puree
1 tsp honey
1/2 sprig fresh thyme
Salt to taste
Black pepper to taste
2 tbs chopped fresh basil

In a skillet, heat the olive oil over medium heat and sauté the onion gently until translucent. Stir in the tomato and red pepper. Add the tomato puree, honey, thyme, salt, and pepper, and simmer for 30 minutes.

Remove the thyme and puree the sauce in a blender. Simmer the sauce, uncovered, until thick. Season to taste with salt and pepper. Add the basil just before serving.

Tomatoes

Tomatoes, like peppers, are highly alkaline forming. They also contain high amounts of potassium and magnesium, which support the kidneys and have a diuretic effect. The antioxidant *lycopene* strengthens the immune system. A thickened tomato sauce is an ideal alkaline-forming spread, and is delicious on toasted bread.

PER PORTION:
140 calories
4 g protein
7 g fat
16 g carbohydrates

Cream Sauce
elegant and very aromatic
with Morels

Serves 2: 3/4 oz dried morels • 1 cup water • 1 shallot • 1 tsp butter • 1 cup vegetable stock • 1/2 tsp cornstarch • 1/4 cup heavy cream • Salt to taste • White pepper to taste

Soak the morels in the water for 8 hours, then wipe clean. Strain the soaking water through a paper coffee filter and reserve. Peel and chop the shallot and sauté it gently in the butter until translucent. Add the morels and simmer briefly. Add the soaking liquid and the stock, and bring to a simmer. Dissolve the cornstarch in the cream. Pour into the mushroom mixture, heat carefully, stirring, until thickened. Season with salt and pepper.

PER PORTION: 116 calories • 1 g protein • 10 g fat • 5 g carbohydrates

Carrot and
a creamy, alkaline-forming topping
Almond Sauce

Serves 2: 7 oz carrots • 1 onion • 1 tbs butter • 1 oz ground almonds • 2 tbs tomato puree • 1/2 cup vegetable stock • Salt to taste • Pepper to taste • Freshly grated nutmeg to taste • 1/4 cup heavy cream • Yeast flakes (optional)

Wash, peel, and grate the carrots. Peel and dice the onion. Sauté the carrots and onion in the butter, until the onion is translucent. Add the almonds, tomato puree, and stock. Season with salt, pepper, and nutmeg and simmer for 5 minutes. Puree in a blender. Stir in the cream and sprinkle with the yeast flakes (if using).

PER PORTION: 212 calories • 4 g protein • 17 g fat • 11 g carbohydrates

Winter Bean

with plenty of vegetable protein

Stew

Chop the tomatoes into small pieces and soak overnight in the water with the beans, bay leaf, and peppercorns.

Serves 2:
3 dried tomatoes
2 1/4 cups water
4 oz dried flageolet beans
1 bay leaf
A few black peppercorns
1 leek
9 oz potatoes
1 clove garlic
Salt to taste
1 oz pumpkin seeds
1-2 tbs pumpkin seed oil
1-2 tbs cider vinegar

In a saucepan, cook the tomatoes and the beans in the soaking water for 30 minutes.

Meanwhile, wash the leek and potatoes. Trim the leek and cut into slices. Peel the potatoes and cut into small dice. Peel and finely chop the garlic.

Add everything to the pan with the beans. Season the stew with salt and cook for about 20 more minutes, until the potatoes are soft.

Toast the pumpkin seeds in a dry nonstick skillet, until golden brown. Add them to the stew with the pumpkin seed oil and cider vinegar. Season with salt.

Seasonal stews

A delicious summer alternative is to make this stew with fresh beans and tomatoes instead of dried ones, and use 1 bell pepper and 2 green onions instead of the leek. In spring, substitute 2-3 baby carrots, and 2 bunches of fresh sorrel for the leek. Or, use 9 oz chopped spinach and 1 chopped onion.

PER PORTION:

398 calories

20 g protein

16 g fat

46 g carbohydrates

Cream of
with potatoes and garlic
Basil Soup

Serves 2: 9 oz potatoes • 1 onion • 1 clove garlic • 1 tbs butter • 2 cups buttermilk • Salt to taste • White pepper to taste • 1-2 tsp arrowroot • 1 bunch fresh basil • 2 tbs sour cream

Wash the potatoes. Peel and finely chop the potatoes, onion, and garlic. In a skillet, sauté the potatoes and onion in the butter until they start to turn brown. Add the buttermilk, season to taste, and simmer for 20 minutes. Mix the arrowroot with 2 tbs water. Add to the potato mixture, bring to a boil, and stir until thickened. Wash the basil, tear off the leaves, and add them to the soup. Carefully puree the mixture and serve garnished with the sour cream.

PER PORTION: 166 calories • 4 g protein • 4 g fat • 28 g carbohydrates

44

Cream of
satisfying and highly alkaline-forming
Pumpkin Soup

Serves 2: 1 1/2 lb pumpkin flesh • 1 onion • 1 tbs olive oil • Salt to taste • Pepper to taste • 1 cup carrot juice • 2 tbs crème fraîche • Ground ginger to taste • Fresh lemon juice to taste • 1 oz dried currants • 1/2 oz roughly chopped pumpkin seeds

Roughly chop the pumpkin flesh. Peel and finely chop the onion. Add both to a saucepan with the oil, season with salt and pepper, and sauté over medium heat until tender. Puree with the carrot juice and crème fraîche. Season with the ginger and lemon juice. Add the currants and pumpkin seeds, heat through, and serve.

PER PORTION: 247 calories • 6 g protein • 13 g fat • 28 g carbohydrates

Vegetable Stock

a tasty base for sauces, stocks, and stews

Peel and chop the onions. Wipe clean the mushrooms and cut into slices. Sauté the onions and mushrooms in a large saucepan without oil until they turn dark.

Wash, trim, and chop the remaining vegetables. Add them to the pan with the water, salt, bay leaves, cloves, peppercorns, and herbs and bring to a boil.

Simmer the vegetables over low heat for 1 hour and let cool. Ideally, let the stock stand overnight in the refrigerator. Pass the liquid through a sieve and season well. The stock will keep for up to 1 week in a sealed container in the refrigerator.

Makes about 1 quart:

2 large onions
4 oz mushrooms
1 carrot
1 stalk celery
1 leek
2-3 ripe tomatoes
5 cups water
1 tsp salt, plus more to taste
2 bay leaves
2 whole cloves
1 tsp black peppercorns
1 sprig fresh rosemary
2 sprigs fresh thyme

Mushrooms

This stock tastes especially good if you chop the mushrooms, sprinkle them with salt, and let them stand for 24 hours. This allows them to ferment, turning brown and highly aromatic. Dried mushrooms have a similar effect. You can sip the stock either hot or cold. For an extremely delicious creamy-style vegetable soup, add carrots, pumpkin, or potatoes, cook, and puree.

PER PORTION:

27 calories

1 g protein

1 g fat

1 g carbohydrates

Vegetable Tempura

gently cooked veggies in a crispy coating

In a small bowl, combine the flours. In another bowl, mix the egg yolk, half egg white, about 1/4 cup of the flour mixture (more if needed), the ice water, salt, and oil to a smooth paste. Refrigerate until ready to use.

Wash and dry the tomatoes. Wipe the mushrooms clean. Wash and trim the leek and cut into finger-width slices. Wash again if necessary. Place the vegetables in the refrigerator for 1 hour.

Coat the vegetables in the remaining flour and then coat them with the batter. Heat about 1 inch of oil in a small saucepan. When hot, add the vegetables and fry until golden brown; drain on paper towels.

Sprinkle lime juice over the vegetables and serve with soy sauce for dipping.

Serves 2:

1/4 cup amaranth flour
1/4 cup spelt flour
1 egg yolk
1/2 egg white
1/2 cup ice water
Salt to taste
1 tsp olive oil
4 oz cherry tomatoes
5 oz small white mushrooms
1 large leek
Vegetable oil
Soy sauce

Deep-fried vegetables

It is important that all the ingredients are cold before frying. Also suitable for tempura: broccoli florets, snow peas or sugar-snap peas, strips of bell pepper, slices of zucchini or eggplant, and asparagus.

PER PORTION:

350 calories

11 g protein

21 g fat

30 g carbohydrates

Curried Potato

with exotic carrot dip

Pancake

Wash, trim, and thinly slice the green onions. Peel and finely chop the garlic, setting one-third aside for the dip. Peel and finely grate the ginger.

Serves 2:
2-3 green onions
2 cloves garlic
1 nut-sized piece fresh ginger
1 1/4 lb potatoes
Salt to taste
White pepper to taste
1-2 tsp curry powder
2 tbs chopped cashew nuts
2 tbs clarified butter or olive oil
7 oz carrots
Grated orange zest to taste
1/2 cup plain yogurt
1 tbs pumpkin seed oil

Wash, peel, and coarsely grate the potatoes. Stir in the green onions, garlic, and ginger. Season well with salt, pepper, and curry powder.

Toast the cashew nuts in a large nonstick skillet with 1 tbs of the clarified butter or oil. Place the potato mixture on top, cover with a lid, and fry gently for 10 minutes. Flip over, adding the remaining 1 tbs clarified butter or oil, and fry until brown.

Meanwhile, peel and puree the carrots. Combine with the remaining garlic, the grated orange zest, yogurt, pumpkin seed oil, and salt and pepper to taste. Cut the potato pancake into serving wedges and serve with the carrot dip.

PER PORTION: 488 calories • 11 g protein • 25 g fat • 54 g carbohydrates

Beet

with buckwheat blinis

Ragout

Mix the flour with the cold water. Stirring constantly, add the warm water, yeast, honey, and 1/2 tsp salt, and let stand for 1 hour.

Wash and peel the beets and cut into 2 inch strips. Peel the onion, cut in half crosswise, and slice thinly. Wash, peel, and halve the apple. Remove the core and cut into segments. Sprinkle with lemon juice. In a saucepan, heat 1 tbs of the oil and add the onion, beets, allspice, and stock and simmer for 10 minutes. Add the apple segments and simmer, uncovered, for 2 minutes. Season the mixture with salt and pepper.

In a skillet, heat 1 tbs of the oil over medium heat. Ladle in three 1/4-cup portions of the blini mixture and fry for 3-4 minutes, until golden brown. Turn the blinis and fry until the other side is golden brown. Remove from the pan and keep warm. Repeat with the remaining blini mixture and oil.

Toast the buckwheat groats in a dry skillet until golden. Place 3 blinis on each plate. Top with some of the beet ragout and a spoonful of sour cream. Garnish with the dill and the buckwheat, and serve immediately.

Serves 2:

3/4 cup buckwheat flour

1/2 cup cold water

1/2 cup warm water (110°F)

1 package active dry yeast

1/2 tsp honey

Salt to taste

14 oz beets

1 medium onion

1 tart apple

2-3 tbs lemon juice

3-4 tbs sunflower oil

Pinch of allspice

1/2 cup vegetable stock

Pepper to taste

3-4 tbs buckwheat groats

2 tbs sour cream

2 tbs chopped fresh dill

PER PORTION: 644 calories • 13 g protein • 30 g fat • 80 g carbohydrates

Stir-Fried

quick and nourishing

Amaranth

In a saucepan, bring the amaranth, lemon grass, and stock to a boil. Reduce the heat and simmer the amaranth for 15 minutes. Wash and trim the green onions and cut into thin slices. Wash and trim the carrots, then peel them and cut into slices. Wipe the mushrooms clean and, depending on size, cut them into four or eight pieces.

Heat the corn oil in a wok over medium heat and stir-fry the almonds until they start to smell aromatic. Add the carrots and stir-fry briefly.

Add the mushrooms, green onions, and bean sprouts and stir-fry for 5 minutes. Add the cooked amaranth and the sesame oil, stir-fry for a moment, and add the soy sauce. Remove the lemon grass and serve immediately.

Serves 2:

1/2 cup amaranth
1 tsp dried lemon grass
1 cup vegetable stock
2 green onions
10 oz baby carrots
7 oz mushrooms
2 tbs corn oil
2 oz skinned almonds
4 oz bean sprouts
1 tbs sesame oil
Soy sauce to taste

 ### Gentle cooking with a wok

A wok is ideal for cooking small portions. Because stir-fried ingredients are cut into small pieces, and the food is cooked quickly, the nutrients are retained. This recipe can also be made with cooked millet, quinoa, or whole-wheat pasta (non-egg) instead of amaranth. Other possible vegetables include Chinese cabbage, broccoli florets, kohlrabi, spinach, beets, bell peppers, and other bean sprouts. Do not cook more than 1 1/4 lb at a time.

PER PORTION:

613 calories

21 g protein

41 g fat

43 g carbohydrates

power

Potato-Apple

with arugula and herbed cheese

Gratin

Wash the potatoes and steam them until tender, about 20-30 minutes. In a saucepan, bring the cream, cheese, and vegetable stock to a boil. Mix the cornstarch with the water, add to the cream mixture, and stir until thick. Season well with salt and pepper and remove from the heat. Wash the arugula and shake it dry. Cut it into pieces and add to the sauce.

Preheat the oven to 400°F. Butter a small baking dish (about 1 quart capacity). Peel and slice the potatoes. Peel and halve the apples and remove the cores. Slice them into segments. Arrange alternate layers of potato and apple in the baking dish and pour the herbed cheese mixture over the top. Sprinkle with the sunflower kernels. Bake the gratin in the middle of the oven for 30 minutes, until golden brown.

Serves 2:

1 lb potatoes
1/4 cup heavy cream
2 tbs herbed cheese, such as Boursin
1 cup vegetable stock
2 tsp cornstarch
2 tbs water
Salt to taste
Pepper to taste
4 oz arugula
Butter for coating the dish
2 small cooking apples
2 oz sunflower kernels

Herbs

Herbs are always alkaline—and that's not all: they are high in vitamins and minerals. Consumed in large quantities, herbs are highly therapeutic and can be used for medicinal purposes. Arugula contains large quantities of mustard oils, which aid the digestion and fight infections.

PER PORTION:

407 calories

11 g protein

19 g fat

51 g carbohydrates

Baked Zucchini on

an appetizing alkaline aid

Tomato Amaranth

Place the amaranth in a saucepan with the tomato juice, a little salt and pepper, and the thyme and bring to a boil. Simmer gently over low heat for 15 minutes. Meanwhile, wash and trim the zucchini. Using a sharp knife, cut the zucchini lengthwise into fan shapes, leaving the stem intact, and gently spread the segments out.

Preheat the oven to 400°F. Grease a small baking dish (1 quart capacity) with a small amount of the oil. Mix the cooked amaranth with the remaining olive oil, pour into the gratin dish, and spread evenly with a spoon. Lay the zucchini fans on top.

Serves 2:
3/4 cup amaranth
1 1/4 cups tomato juice
Salt to taste
White pepper to taste
1/2 tsp dried thyme
1 lb baby zucchini
1-2 tbs olive oil
3 tbs ground hazelnuts
3 tbs freshly grated
Parmesan cheese

Mix the hazelnuts with the Parmesan and sprinkle over the zucchini. Place the dish in the center of the oven and bake for 20 minutes, until golden brown.

PER PORTION: 584 calories • 22 g protein • 31 g fat • 58 g carbohydrates

Fresh Plum
with plum compote and hazelnuts
Dumplings

Wash the potatoes and steam them until tender, about 20-30 minutes. Peel the
potatoes while still hot and push them through a potato ricer. Let stand for a few
minutes to drive off the steam. Carefully mix the riced potatoes
with a pinch of salt, the flour, and as much potato flour as
necessary so that the mixture holds together, but is still very soft.
Wash the plums. Select the 12 best and dry them. Carefully
remove the stones, then push the plums together so that they
appear to be intact. Divide the dough into 12 equal pieces, press a
plum into the center of each piece, and gently roll into a ball.
Halve the remaining plums and remove the stones. Very gently
simmer the plums with 1/2 tsp of the cinnamon and the water
until tender. Stir 2 tbs of the maple syrup into the compote and chill.

In another saucepan, bring a large amount of salted water to a boil. Drop the
dumplings in the water and simmer, uncovered, for 10 minutes, until they rise to the
top. Remove with a slotted spoon and drain.

In a skillet, heat the butter over medium heat and sauté the nuts until golden. Add the
remaining 1/2 tsp cinnamon and toss the plum dumplings in this mixture. Drizzle them
with the remaining 2 tbs syrup and serve with the compote.

Serves 2:
1 lb baking potatoes
Salt to taste
3 tbs flour
2-3 tbs potato flour
14 oz small fresh plums
1 tsp ground cinnamon
2 tbs water
4 tbs maple syrup
2 tbs butter
2 tbs finely chopped hazelnuts

PER PORTION: 538 calories • 8 g protein • 14 g fat • 94 g carbohydrates

Red Currant
light and refreshing
Sorbet Float

Wash and sort the red currants, remove them from the stalks, and drain. Puree the berries and press through a sieve into a freezerproof bowl. Stir in the maple syrup. Place the mixture in the freezer, stirring every 30 minutes, until frozen.

Transfer the sorbet to the refrigerator about 30 minutes before serving. Stir the sorbet well, divide among two glasses, and top with sparkling water.

Serves 2:
9 oz fresh red currants
Scant 1/2 cup maple syrup
Pinch of ground cinnamon
Sparkling water

✱ Fruity desserts

These dishes are alkaline forming, provided they do not contain large amounts of dairy products, eggs, white flour, gelatin, or sugar. Use agar-agar instead of gelatin, cornstarch or arrowroot instead of flour, cocoa powder instead of chocolate, and honey, maple syrup, or dried fruit puree instead of refined sugar.

PER PORTION:
216 calories
1 g protein
1 g fat
51 g carbohydrates

Chocolate

sweetened with dried dates

Pudding

Serves 2: 8 dried pitted dates • 2 1/2 cups whole milk • 5 tbs unsweetened cocoa powder

• 2 tbs cornstarch • 2 tbs water

Wash the dates and puree with a blender. Place in a saucepan, and gradually add the milk and cocoa powder. Bring to a boil, stirring constantly. Mix the cornstarch with the water, stir into the cocoa mixture, and simmer gently for 1 minute over low heat. Divide among 2 dessert bowls and chill until ready to serve.

PER PORTION: 314 calories • 13 g protein • 13 g fat • 51 g carbohydrates

Tropical

with lime juice and pineapple

Jelly

Serves 2: 1 small fresh pineapple • 3 oranges • 1 lime • Scant 1 tsp agar-agar • 2-3 tbs honey

Peel the pineapple and cut into slices. Remove the woody core and cut the slices into pieces. Peel and divide 2 of the oranges into segments. Squeeze the juice from the remaining orange and the lime. Add enough water to the juice to make 1 cup of liquid. Remove 2-3 tbs juice and mix with the agar-agar. Bring the remaining juice mixture to a boil, stir in the agar-agar, and boil for 1-2 minutes. Stir in the honey and fruit, pour into a mold, and chill for at least 4 hours.

PER PORTION: 162 calories • 1 g protein • 1 g fat • 38 g carbohydrates

Semifrozen
Fruit Pudding
with berried-banana puree

Combine the yogurt, vanilla, honey, and lemon zest and stir until smooth and creamy. Add the agar-agar and let stand for 15 minutes. Then, simmer the mixture gently in a small saucepan for 2-3 minutes and let cool. Stir in the egg yolk when the mixture starts to set at the edges. In a bowl, whip the cream until stiff peaks form, and fold into the pudding mixture.

Line a small mold or dish with aluminum foil (shiny side up). Grease the foil. Pour the mixture into the prepared mold and place in the freezer for at least 6 hours or up to overnight.

To serve, carefully remove the pudding from the mold, discard the foil, and let the dessert stand for 30 minutes.

Meanwhile, make the sauce: Squeeze the juice from the lemon. Peel and slice the banana and puree with the lemon juice and honey. Add the banana puree to the berries in a bowl. Serve the pudding with the berried-banana puree.

Serves 2:
1/2 cup plain yogurt
1/2 tsp vanilla extract
2 tbs clover honey
1 tsp grated lemon zest
1 tsp agar-agar
1 egg yolk
1/2 cup heavy cream
Vegetable oil for greasing the dish
For the sauce:
1 lemon
1 banana
2-3 tbs honey
1/2 pint fresh raspberries

PER PORTION: 493 calories • 7 g protein • 23 g fat • 67 g carbohydrates

INDEX

Acid-alkaline balance   2-7

Almond
        and carrot sauce   41
        and potato spread   16

Amaranth   20
        stir-fried   50
        tomato, baked zucchini on   53

Apple-potato gratin   52
Arugula and wild rice salad   23

Asparagus
        and tomato salad   27
        dip, creamy   37

Basil, cream of, soup   44
Beans, kidney, with dandelion salad   25
Beet ragout   49

Berry(ies)
        fresh, sprouted muesli with   21
        milkshake   12

Bread, spelt and potato   15
Buckwheat-stuffed tomatoes   35

Cinnamon, pear milkshake with   13
Cocktail, potato and tomato   13
Cream sauce with morels   41

Dandelion salad with kidney beans   25

Dips   37

Dumplings
        fresh plum   55
        gnocchi with tomatoes   39

Fennel   28
        roasted, with exotic mushrooms   28

Fruit
        honeyed fresh   11
        mixed, granola   20
        mixed, puree   17
        uncooked mixed, jam   17

Ginger and nettle tisane with licorice   12
Gnocchi with tomatoes   39

Grains   18

Granola, mixed fruit   20
Gratin, potato-apple   52

Herbs   52

Jam, uncooked mixed-fruit   17

Lettuce, butter, and quinoa salad   24
Licorice, ginger and nettle tisane with   12

Milkshake
        berry   12
        pear, with cinnamon   13

Millet and spelt, muesli with   18
Morels with cream sauce   41

Muesli
        with spelt and millet   18
        sprouted, fresh berries with   21

Mushrooms   45
        cream sauce with morels   41
        exotic, roasted fennel with   28

Nettle and ginger tisane with licorice   12

Pancake, curried potato   48
Pasta salad, green   32

Abbreviations:
tsp = teaspoon
tbs = tablespoon

Pear milkshake with cinnamon 13

Pepper(s) **29**
   marinated 29
   red, and tomato sauce 40

Plum, fresh, dumplings 55

Potato(es) **16**
   and almond spread 16
   -apple gratin 52
   pancake, curried 48
   and spelt bread 15
   and tomato cocktail 13

Power week eating plan 8-9

Pumpkin
   cream of, soup 44
   salsa verde 36

Quinoa **33**
   and butter lettuce salad 24
   salad with creamy vinaigrette 33

Radish dip, spicy 36
Ragout, beet 49
Rice, wild, and arugula salad 23

Salsa verde, pumpkin 36

Sauce
   carrot and almond 41
   cream, with morels 41

Seeds, sprouted 21

Soup (see also stew)
   cream of basil 44
   cream of pumpkin 44

Spelt
   and millet, muesli with 18

   and potato bread 15

Spinach **32**

Spread
   mixed fruit puree 17
   potato and almond 16
   uncooked mixed-fruit jam 17

Stew(s)
   beet ragout 49
   seasonal 42
   winter bean 42

Stock, vegetable **45**

Tempura, vegetable 47
Tisane, ginger and nettle, with licorice 12

Tomato(es) **40**
   amaranth, baked zucchini on 53
   and asparagus salad 27
   buckwheat-stuffed 35
   gnocchi with 39
   and potato cocktail 13
   and red pepper sauce 40

Vegetable
   salad, provençal 30
   stock 45
   tempura 47

Vinaigrette, creamy, with quinoa salad 33

Wok cooking **50**

Zucchini, baked, on tomato amaranth 53

Published originally under the title
SÄURE BASEN BALANCE: Topfit und
gesund mit Leichtigkeit

©1999 Gräfe und Unzer Verlag GmbH,
Munich
English translation copyright for the US
edition: © 2000 Silverback Books, Inc.

Editors: Ina Schröter, Jennifer Newens, CCP
Readers' department: Dipl. oec. troph.
Maryna Zimdars, Vené Franco
Layout and design: Heinz Kraxenberger
Production: Helmut Giersberg,
Shanti Nelson
Photos: FoodPhotography Eising, Munich
Typeset: Easy Pic Library, Munich
Reproduction: Repro Schmidt, Dornbirn
Printing: Appl, Wemding
Binding: Sellier, Freising

ISBN: 1-930603-05-3

Caution

The techniques and recipes in this book are
to be used at the reader's sole discretion
and risk. Always consult a doctor before
beginning a new eating plan.

Dagmar von Cramm
Studied ecotrophology, and after graduation
began to practice nutritional theory in
cooking. The mother of three sons, she has
been a freelance food journalist since 1984.
She has been a member of the Presiding
Committee of the German Society for
Nutrition since 1996.

Susie M. and **Pete Eising** have studios in
Munich and Kennebunkport, Maine/USA.
They studied at the Munich Academy of
Photography, where they established their
own studio for food photography in 1991.

For this book:
Photographic layout:
Martina Görlach
Food styling:
Monika Schuster

Our thanks for their support with the
photography go to:
ASA (Höhr-Grenzhausen)
Boss elitaire (Balingen)
LSA (London)
WMF (Geislingen/Steige)

SILVERBACK

BOOKS, INC.

www.silverbackbooks.com